From the Foot of the Cross

Prayers for Those Who Watch and Wait
with Those They Love

John Elliston

FROM THE FOOT OF THE CROSS
Prayers for Those Who Watch and Wait with Those They Love

Copyright © 2005 John P. Elliston
Original edition published in English under the title FROM THE
FOOT OF THE CROSS by Kevin Mayhew Ltd, Buxhall, England.
This edition copyright © Fortress Press 2019

All rights reserved. Except for brief quotations in critical articles or
reviews, no part of this book may be reproduced in any manner
without prior written permission from the publisher. Email
copyright@augsburgfortress.org or write to Permissions, Fortress
Press, PO Box 1209, Minneapolis, MN 55440-1209.

Scripture quotations are from *The Revised Standard Version of the
Bible*, copyright © 1946, 1952 and 1971 by the Division of Christian
Education of the National Council of Churches in the USA. Used
by permission.

Cover image: Photo by Nitish Meena on Unsplash
Cover design: Joe Reinke

Print ISBN: 978-1-5064-5920-2

Contents

Acknowledgments		4
About the Author		4
Preface		5
Introduction		7
1.	Stay Here, and Keep Watch with Me ...	9
2.	Tears	11
3.	Laughter	13
4.	Uncertainty	15
5.	The Place of Decision	19
6.	Loneliness	23
7.	Memories	27
8.	What Love Can Do	29
9.	Between Life and Death	31
10.	And It Was Night	33
11.	Walking Away	35
12.	Into a Journey of Grief	37

Acknowledgments

I humbly acknowledge within these pages all those people whose journey through pain I have been privileged to both share and observe in the course of my work as a Baptist minister. It is they, more than anything else, who convince me that the grace of God is sufficient for all our needs.

About the Author

The Reverend Dr. John Elliston is a Baptist minister, currently working at Grange Road Baptist Church in Darlington, England. He has written a number of books of prayers including *Here in our Midst, Footprints on Sand, From the Depths, Walking With Pain,* and *Walking the Way of the Cross: Prayers For Your Personal Journey.*

Preface

At some time in our lives, many of us find ourselves at the bedside of someone we love who is coming to the end of his or her life. It may be in the setting of a hospital, where our chief role is that of visitor, or it may be at home, where as a caregiver we attend to the needs of someone who is terminally ill. Whatever the setting, it involves a lot of watching and waiting. The prayers contained in this collection are watching and waiting prayers. They represent the struggle to pray through—and to find God within—the watching and the waiting hours.

Dame Cicely Saunders, the founder of St. Christopher's Hospice, once observed that the principle lesson the dying teach us is that suffering is only intolerable if nobody cares. To pray, however incoherently, is to care.

Introduction

In October 1998, I sat beside a bed in St. Christopher's Hospice in South London as my father came to the end of his life. Five weeks later I was back in the same ward, sitting beside an adjacent bed to the first as my mother died of secondary cancer. For both my parents, death came slowly. There were times of lucidity and times of withdrawal for each of them, times of peace and times of pain, which meant that I, and those who watched with me, were on a kind of emotional rollercoaster, rising on waves of hope and sinking in troughs of despair.

In the course of the events recalled above I spent a great deal of time at the bedside, watching and waiting, trying to respond to both verbalized and observed need. There is a limit to the number of times one can moisten lips, stroke a forehead, express love. Like Mary at the foot of the cross, I knew that there was very little of practical use I could do to ease the pain of the moment; all I could do was to be there.

This booklet is for all those who sit beside hospital beds and who know their own powerlessness, but who know, too, that they are where Christ asks them to be.

1

Stay Here, and Keep Watch with Me . . .

> *Then Jesus went with them to a place called Gethsemane, and he said to his disciples, "Sit here, while I go yonder and pray." And taking with him Peter and the two sons of Zebedee, he began to be sorrowful and troubled. Then he said to them, "My soul is very sorrowful, even to death; remain here, and watch with me."*
>
> Matthew 26:36–8

Lord, it is the watching hour,
when love is called to witness the beloved's pain,
to know the angry yearning for a different day,
and to feel the terrible powerlessness
of flesh and blood before the final enemy.
Grant me the strength to be faithful in watching,
courage to endure when tempted to turn away,
and grace to keep a truthful vigil and not, as your disciples,
to surrender to sleep.
Help me to share, insofar as it is possible to share,
this final human journey,
so that above everything
my beloved knows that I am here.

John Elliston

Lord, it is the waiting hour,
when clock time gives way to the body's time,
and the tick of passing seconds
is marked by the uncertainty of the next heartbeat
and the faltering rhythm of tired lungs.
Grant me patience in waiting,
so that I may gratefully accept
the sacrament of the given moment,
penetrate its meaning, and not become distracted
by either yesterday's memories
or by a hope that the ordeal will soon be over.
In my presence by the bedside, may I be truly
　present.

Lord, it is the healing hour,
when little by little,
all that endures is gathered into your love,
when the spirit is divested of the flesh that has
served it so faithfully,
and the glory of humanity is transfigured into a
　new humanity
that we have glimpsed in you.
Grant me faith,
so that through the pain of this vigil,
I may see through the darkness to the coming dawn,
may glimpse the future that you have prepared,
and may understand that time must be surrendered
before there can begin a life in your eternity.

Amen.

2

Tears

> *But Ruth said, "Entreat me not to leave you or to return from following you; for where you go I will go, and where you lodge I will lodge; your people shall be my people, and your God my God; where you die I will die, and there will I be buried. May the Lord do so to me and more also if even death parts me from you."*
>
> Ruth 1:16–17

We do not need to ask God's forgiveness for our tears. Dying is a departure with a permanence we cannot, in this life, penetrate. Even if faith can see a new day, the fact remains that it is here, in this life, that we have both formed our relationships and given them substance in touch, in the spoken word, and in the meeting of eyes; death steals the substantial.

Gracious God,
on the edge of tears, sustain me,
for loss is cutting away my heart like a surgeon's
    knife,
and I am not anesthetized against the pain.
I want to be strong, to hide my vulnerability,
lest the weight of a single tear
disturb the delicate balance between life and death,

and tip my beloved into a deeper night.
And yet, tears are all I have,
the holy water of love's consecration,
a sacrament that washes, and heals,
and gives me the freedom to be.
Lord, thank you for the gift of tears . . .

> an outward sign of inner grief that joins me to
> the one I love,
> a living stream that flows as a river
> to a Father's heart,
> a merciful outpouring that comforts
> through uncertain and lonely hours.

May I never seek forgiveness that I shed them,
nor deny that I have cried,
for tears are my anguish and lament,
the only words that pain can speak over this lost
  Jerusalem.

Reassure me, weeping Christ,
that, as death steals what eye can see and hands
  can touch,
as it silently infiltrates the very fibers of the human
  frame,
and turns the living clay to silence and dust,
love remains the greater power,
that in the end all is triumph,
and that above all,
it is OK to cry.

Amen.

3

Laughter

Even in laughter the heart is sad, and the end of joy is grief.

Proverbs 14:13

It seems something of a paradox that reference should be made to laughter in the context of a bedside vigil. Surely, it will be protested, the gravity of the situation demands something more somber. Death, however, is not devoid of humor, and to allow laughter a place within it is a way of integratting the end of a person's life into the totality of what it means to be human.

Lord, there is something rather comical
about our seriousness at the moment of parting . . .

> the weighty and considered words
> that might be the last,
> the line-marked brows of deep concern,
> the measured silences borne of human pain.

Like clowns, treading the boundary between
  laughter and tears,

John Elliston

we act the part,
unable to believe the truth of what is happening,
hoping against hope that when the performance is
 over,
death's make-up will be removed,
and all will be well.

Lord, the last laugh belongs to you,
for Christ has removed the sting of death,
transforming the end into a new beginning,
transfiguring the place of tears into a place of joy,
supplanting the emptiness of mourning
with the fullness of resurrection.

Lord, may the echoes of that holy laughter
be heard at the foot of my cross as well as in the
 Easter garden,
so that the finality of losing
might be mediated by an anticipated tomorrow,
and the coming journey through grief
might be suffused with a word of hope.

God of my laughter, God of my tears,
God of my time, God of my eternity,
God of my life, God of my death,
in you I trust.

Amen.

4

Uncertainty

> *When Isaac was old and his eyes were dim so that he could not see, he called Esau his older son, and said to him, "My son"; and he answered, "Here I am." He said, "Behold, I am old; I do not know the day of my death."*
>
> Genesis 27:1–2

On four occasions over a period of about two years I was summoned to a hospital bed because my father was, according to the doctors, close to death. In my work as a minister there have been many other "false alarms." Equally, there have been times when, having been assured that death will be some time away, I have left a hospital ward only to discover that the person died before I had reached the hospital ground floor. The time of a person's death belongs only to God; it is a privilege to share it, but not a right. Moreover, if someone we love dies alone, in spite of our best efforts, we should not close our mind to the possibility that that was how he or she wanted it—a last act of love.

Lord, even as journey's end seems to be in sight,
the road remains unpredictable;

John Elliston

everyone is urging me to prepare myself,
to summon the necessary courage for a
   final farewell,
and I am prepared . . . as prepared as I ever will be.
Yet even as I witness for myself the physical
   changes . . .

   the slowing and irregular pulse,
   the shallow breathing,
   the face that I know so well apparently closing in
   on itself,
   into a shape I do not recognize.

Still I fantasize that in this minute (or the next)
my beloved will rise like some latter-day Tabitha,
and speak, and laugh, and cry,
over all that he [she] has put me through.

Lord, the time and the manner of death is not in
   human hands;
it is your gift, the final healing of love by love,
the closing of this earthly chapter
that the human story may further unfold.

As I watch and wait,
may I have the consolation of knowing
that death is not beyond your love,
that your providence is as active in the body's
   demise
as it is the history of nations
or the movement of the stars,

and may I have the faith to believe
that even as I now feel I am losing all there is to
  lose,
nothing that matters will be lost.

Gracious God, in all the uncertainties of this vigil,
may I find certainty in you,
and where my faith falters,
help me to trust you.

Amen.

5

The Place of Decision

Whether we think of our own death or that of someone we love, we hope that when it comes, death will come quickly. In reality, however, for most people death is not an event but a managed process. Modern medicine has not only extended our lives, it has given us the power to manage our deaths, so that the transition from life to death depends upon human decision making. The question is: "Who decides?"

Sometimes, of course, a person, knowing that he or she is drawing near to death, makes a conscious decision not to be subjected to intensive intervention for the purpose of prolonging life. This might take the form of an expressed wish or a living will. More often, however, an individual is too sick, too removed from the needs of the moment, to make such a decision. It then falls to "those who watch and wait," the doctors and the next of kin.

From the perspective of the relatives (if not of the medical staff), the complexity of the issue and the time given to make the decision are frequently disproportionate to its consequences. In practice, choices have to be made in the context of a single interview with a hospital consultant. The enormity of the decision, its moral, ethical, and spiritual implications, become lost to the needs of the moment.

Sometimes they are lost forever, sometimes they come back to haunt.

Holy Father,
as it was for Mary at the foot of the cross,
our waiting and our watching
is an experience that is double edged . . .

> like a sword that pierces the heart,
> and like the joy that greets the coming dawn.

We long for life to continue
as we hold on to what our hands can touch,
and, as we continue to behold what our eyes can recognize,
we long for death,
so that pain and fear may be no more,
and the waiting hours be fulfilled by what in the end will be.

In the economy of grace and the shadow of your love,
you have taught us that all things have their time—

> there is a time for laughter and a time for tears,
> a time for rebellion and time for acceptance,
> a time for affirming life and a time for
> surrendering to death.

Help us not to divorce any of the "times" from your love,

but rather, may we see them within the richness of
   your giving,
so that, however the process of decision weighs
   upon our minds,
we may know that there is no human experience
in which we can depart from your presence,
or feel that, in Christ, you do not understand.

Lord, in the uncertainty of tomorrow,
in the interplay of life meeting death and death
   meeting life,
in the longing for today
and the promise of tomorrow,
may we have confidence that,
though unseen and though unrecognized,
yet in divine providence you are guiding,
and the decision that, in love, we make today,
in the cold light of tomorrow, we will still see as
   loving.
So may we be delivered from regret,
and have the faith to believe
that within the turmoil of our minds,
within the restlessness of thought
and the frenetic questioning of decisions made,
your will has been done.

Amen.

6

Loneliness

My heart is in anguish within me, the terrors of death have fallen upon me. Fear and trembling come upon me, and horror overwhelms me.
Psalm 55:4–5

As Mary the mother of Jesus stood at the foot of the cross, she is traditionally believed to have remained silent. But there can be little doubt that, as her son died, her body yearned to hold him and that in her mind were formed all the things she wanted to say but which somehow could not now be said. To be unable to hold the one you love, and to be unable to articulate one's deepest thoughts, feels like nothing other than being totally alone.

It was the loneliness of my own bedside vigil that most surprised me. It was a kind a dress rehearsal for the isolation and the loneliness of grief.

Lord, beside this bed I keep my vigil,
occupying the passing hours with memory,
reaching out to touch,
to stroke an arm as a sign that I want to share,
to say again and again words that were yesterday
 so difficult,

but today, as I watch and wait, are all I have to give:
I love you.

I love you . . .
words that mask a passion that language cannot
    bear,
mechanically uttered,
replacing the latent scream,
as together we are drawn into the somber injustice
of losing everything that really matters . . .
    each other.

Lord, to watch and wait is a lonely calling,
not lonely in a physical sense,
because others watch and wait with me,
but within, I am alone.
It is as if no one has traveled this way before;
I am a pioneer,
an explorer of an uncharted and unforgiving terrain
that will claim my life in grief
as certainly as it will claim my beloved's life in death.

Lord, Mary kept this lonely vigil;
held in the place of pain by a mother's love,
watching as I watch,
waiting as I wait,
unable to close her eyes
or turn away from a suffering she could neither
    ease nor change.
Grant me Mary's courage,
that alone as I now feel,

my mind will hold firm to the simple but eternal
  truth
that has guided all my days—
I am enfolded in divine love.

Amen.

7

Memories

> *Many will praise his understanding, and it will never be blotted out; his memory will not disappear, and his name will live through all generations.* Sirach 39:9

To be beside the bedside of someone who is dying can be likened to standing on a seashore at the point where the sand meets the sea. It is the interface between this life and the life to come. Before lies the hope of tomorrow; behind lie the memories of yesterday. The one thing that bedside vigils offer, by definition, is plenty of time to remember.

Gracious God,
all that I hold of this fading life is held in
   yesterday;
the precious memories of love, and laughter,
and shared experience,
the dreams we had in common,
and the hopes—
some fulfilled,
and others slipping through our fingers
as death draws near.

John Elliston

Lord, we have been so close in life,
that in this death part of me is also dying;
I am diminished because he [she] will share my
   journey no longer,
and I feel loss, because the relationship between us
   has, in part at least,
told me who I am.

Thank you for memory . . .

   the things that now come flooding back
   as we share these last precious moments,
   the togetherness that lives on within me
   that nothing can take away,
   the indestructible kinship of faith, hope, and love
   that guards the entrance of eternal sleep.

Lord, I believe that nothing in love is lost,
that in death everything we have been
   and all that we are
is gathered up in love,
and so in love is held every memory
by which our lives are linked.
Hold me in that love,
so that when death comes and robs me of everything
   that really matters,
the joy of yesterday will not be surrendered in
   forgetfulness.

Amen.

8

What Love Can Do

> *Set me as a seal upon your heart, as a seal upon your arm; for love is strong as death, jealousy is cruel as the grave. Its flashes are flashes of fire, a most vehement flame. Many waters cannot quench love, neither can floods drown it.*
>
> Song of Solomon 8:6

The most common context for the bedside vigil is a hospital or hospice, though a growing realization that death is not a medical but a social phenomenon has led to a growing respect for a person's wish to die at home. Whether in hospital or at home, those who sit by the bedside are predominantly spectators of a process that is both natural, and in essence, solitary.

Lord, love can do but small things now—

> no grand gestures,
> no promises of a shared tomorrow,
> no expensive gifts to express through bounty
> the depths of what I feel.

All I can do is hold a hand,
wipe a brow,
and moisten parched lips with cool,
   refreshing water.

John Elliston

They are futile acts, inconsequential acts,
but they are all I have left,
and soon they, too, will cease to have any meaning.

Lord, I want to truly share this dying,
to be on the inside,
not as a stranger hovering on the boundaries,
so near but so far away,
but as a lover,
feeling in my own flesh this futile crucifixion.
And yet, you deny me,
for death, like birth, is a journey that must be
   made alone,
an ultimate reminder of what love cannot do.

Lord, in moments when words do not flow
and the soul is tongue-tied by grief's deeper pain,
remind me of the Spirit's voice,
the groaning, inarticulate language of love,
that both unites me with the person I love,
and brings my prayer to you.

Amen.

9

Between Life and Death

As the body shuts down, a person becomes increasingly less a part of this life. Meaningful communication ceases, the eyes close, and the face somehow seems to turn inward as consciousness gives way to unconsciousness. It is a state that has been likened to fetal consciousness just prior to birth: the unborn child is between two worlds, the world of the womb and a world beyond the mother, which through nine months of gestation is known by intimation. So it is with the person who is dying; there comes a point when they are between worlds; the world of time and the world of an eternal rest.

Lord our God,
in the waiting hours,
in the fear-filled landscape between life and death,
where every breath, so carefully observed,
cries out for interpretation,
and every movement asks, "Is this the last?"
Remind me that death is your gift,
that a new dawn comes only at your command,
that as in the beginning you gave,
so at the last you will receive.

John Elliston

Lord our God,
in the watching hours,
grant me the faith to believe beyond what is seen,
that within the body disfigured by pain and decay,
there is a child full of laughter,
a spirit that roams free,
and love that transcends the process of dying.

Watching and waiting God,
be not far from me now,
that when the pain of travail has passed
and the earthly body has been clothed in immortality,
you will be there, like an expectant Father,
waiting to lift the newborn
into your all-loving arms.

Amen.

10

And It Was Night

> *Nicodemus also, who had at first come to him by night, came bringing a mixture of myrrh and aloes, about a hundred pounds' weight. They took the body of Jesus, and bound it in linen cloths with the spices, as is the burial custom of the Jews.*
> John 19:39–40

In the end, the body once so full of energy and life falls silent. Like silence between waves as they break upon the seashore, there is nothing dramatic or frightening about it. A moment ago, we were watching and waiting with life, and now we watch and wait with death.

God our Father,
confronted by a silence we cannot penetrate,
embraced by a darkness that knows not light,
surrounded by a sadness that seeks consolation,
we surrender this life to you in the vulnerability
  of faith—

  faith that extends beyond what is seen,
  touched, and felt,
  faith full of longing,

John Elliston

faith that rebels against the reality of today
and reaches out for a new dawn,
where silence is gathered into the song of creation,
darkness is interpreted by love,
and sadness finds consolation
in the mystery of your presence.

Holy Father,
in this grief, grant me the courage
not to surrender the faith I have,
but to hold on to that which I know,
so that I am held within your hands,
so that nothing in life is wasted,
and so that out of the unfathomable mystery
   of death
comes everlasting life.
And for the rest,
help me to trust you.

Amen.

11

Walking Away

> *But Mary stood weeping outside the tomb, and as she wept she stooped to look into the tomb; and she saw two angels in white, sitting where the body of Jesus had lain, one at the head and one at the feet. They said to her, "Woman, why are you weeping?" She said to them, "Because they have taken away my Lord, and I do not know where they have laid him." Saying this, she turned round and saw Jesus standing, but she did not know that it was Jesus.*
>
> John 20:11–14

When someone we love dies, sooner or later we have to leave the body behind and walk away. Leaving, we know that we will never again return to this place, while at the same time we fantasize that it has all been just a dream, and that the body so carefully laid out will rise and call our name.

Lord, it feels like an abandonment,

   to simply walk away,
   to leave a body that still holds the warmth of life,
   to let go of a hand so familiar to hold,

yet, like the angel's voice on Easter morning,
something within me declares a rising,
and the person I have known so well
is no longer to be found in flesh and blood.

"He is not here, but risen," they said,
and grief-filled disciples were released to joy,
a mysterious joy, a healing joy,
not the recovered joy of yesterday,
but the pristine joy of a new tomorrow.

Lord, as I walk away from this death,
shudder, and retreat into incredulity,
remind me that love can do no more;
remind me that this life has been taken into you;
remind me that though I leave behind a body
I will carry him [her] within me,
   wherever I go.

Amen.

12

Into a Journey of Grief

For everything there is a season, and a time for every matter under heaven:

  a time to be born, and a time to die;
  a time to plant, and a time to pluck up what is planted;
  a time to kill, and a time to heal;
  a time to break down, and a time to build up;
  a time to weep, and a time to laugh;
  a time to mourn, and a time to dance;
  a time to cast away stones, and a time to gather stones together;
  a time to embrace, and a time to refrain from embracing.

Ecclesiastes 3:1–5

If death robs us of those we love, grief is the process whereby we learn to recover what death has stolen and live with those we love in new ways.

God our Father,
our dying is part of your love,

a mystery beyond that embraces us,
a gift in which we are enclosed,
an ending, which is also a beginning;
and yet, for those who are left,

it is painful separation,
it is the emptiness of grief,
it is bewilderment that feels like fear.

Be with me now, and in the days to come,
strengthen and sustain me in faith,
confirm and renew my hope,
for the journey before me is long,
and the way ahead is dark.

Help me, gracious Lord,
to weave this death into the tapestry of my life,
so that it provokes neither anger nor regret.
May I glimpse within it not the black hood of a
  reaper,
but the healing hands of love,

recreating what is broken,
renewing what is old,
redeeming what is lost,

so that as I draw nearer to my own departing,
I may do so unafraid.

Amen.